Our
Balanced Attack

Howard Culbertson, D.Min., is a veteran Nazarene missionary, having served both in Europe and the Caribbean. Following almost a decade in Italy, the Culbertsons assumed responsibilities in Haiti in 1984. Here Dr. Culbertson became the mission director, and under his administration the church experienced explosive growth.

Previous titles from his pen include *Mr. Missionary: I Have a Question* and *The Kingdom Strikes Back*. Howard, his wife, Barbara, and children, Matthew, 19, and Rachel, 16, live in Bethany, Okla., where Howard serves as missionary-in-residence at Southern Nazarene University.

Our Balanced Attack

How Nazarenes Finance
World Evangelism

by
HOWARD CULBERTSON

NAZARENE PUBLISHING HOUSE
Kansas City, Missouri

10   9   8   7   6   5   4   3   2   1

Contents

☰ 1 ☰

Football and Missions Giving

If I'm in my car on an autumn Saturday afternoon, I'll turn on the radio and hunt for a football game broadcast. It's a habit I developed growing up in Oklahoma.

Oklahoma is a football-crazy state. It doesn't have a professional football team. No matter. The University of Oklahoma regularly wins its conference championship. They've been crowned national champions several times. Not long ago, a player from Oklahoma State University, Barry Sanders, won the Heisman trophy given each year to the best college football player in the United States. Teams from Oklahoma universities often play in postseason bowl games.

Because of where I grew up, I caught football fever. I spent autumn Saturday afternoons listening to the Oklahoma Sooner Football Network. I dreamed about being a great football player. Alas, I never did play on a school team. The only time I got out of the bleachers and onto a playing field was playing my trumpet in the band. Along the way, I did play a lot of sandlot football. Of course, my dream of being a great player was unrealistic. Usually I was the shortest kid on the playground. Without question I was the skinniest. So they always chose me last. Still, whether as a player or a spectator, I have always loved football. I'm from Oklahoma, and Oklahoma is a football-crazy state.

There are some important things you should know about football. One is that you don't win championships depending on a single player. You've got to have a balanced attack. That means using the skills of a variety of players. Consistent winning takes a team effort. "Balanced attack" also refers to the way you play the game. Football teams don't win game after game by throwing passes on every play. They will not win by always running the ball. Winners balance their offense with a mix of running and passing plays. A real championship team will be further balanced by having a top defensive strategy.

What does all this have to do with missions? Well, let me first give an example of a missions program that tried to operate without a balanced attack. Not long ago a well-known American televangelist confessed to grievous moral lapses. At the height of his glory, money flowed toward him like iron filings attracted to a magnet. With some of that money he bankrolled most of his denomination's mission work in Haiti. Among the things he paid for were hot lunches in 100 elementary schools. Then, one Sunday evening on television he confessed to immorality.

By Monday morning a full-blown scandal had erupted around him. He seemed briefly contrite. Then he plunged ahead, using everything sent in by faithful supporters to keep his headquarters open (and personal airplane flying). Anticipating that donations would fall off after his confession, he called Haiti that first week to shut down the lunch programs. On payday two weeks later Haitian teachers in "his" schools got empty envelopes. We had missionary friends supported directly by this television preacher. Their total reliance on his money brought their work crashing to a halt. Within days after the scandal broke, these missionaries packed up to go home. Without his financial support their ministry had collapsed like a football team who had depended too much on one star player who breaks his leg.

Nazarene missionaries are different. The funds for our global ministries are raised in several different ways. For me, football's balanced attack makes a great illustration of how Nazarenes look for resources to fulfill Christ's Great Commission. We Nazarenes don't depend on one person giving all the money. We use several different fund-raising avenues. We appeal to the young and old, to the rich and poor. Sometimes we appeal to the emotions, sometimes to a rational sense of careful stewardship.

The results are impressive. Flying in the face of the selfish materialism gripping much of our world, Nazarenes give more money for missions than many larger denominations. As a result, we have more missionaries than the United Methodist church, a denomination with 10 times our membership.

The longer I'm involved in Nazarene missions outreach, the more convinced I become of the soundness of our balanced fund-raising strategy. What is so special about it? Well, to begin with, ongoing expenses like missionary salaries and hospital supplies are underwritten by a budget system. This budget—our General Budget—provides continuity for our missions outreach. Through economic boom and bust, through the poundings Satan may give us, we'll be fulfilling our divine mandate, thanks to General Budget. To balance out a rather mundane-sounding budget system, some of our other fund-raising ventures encourage spontaneity, appealing to the emotions. These include offerings to open new countries, to buy horses for rural pastors, to help disaster victims, and to build buildings.

Aided by funds raised through our balanced attack, we Nazarenes have been able to move through lots of doors God has opened in front of us. We've planted districts of thriving holiness churches on six continents. In 1983 we celebrated 75 years as a denomination. That year we urged churches to *overpay* their General Budget share. Those overpayments helped us enter several countries: Burma, the Azores, Kenya, Suriname, and Botswana. Adding these to the list of areas already penetrated gave us a total of 74 world areas, just one short of our diamond anniversary goal of 75 (one world area for each year since the 1908 Pilot Point merger).

Now, less than a decade later, we're in more than 95 world areas. Fueling such global outreach is a diversified fund-raising system combining the best of emotional spontaneity with long-term commitment. That's what this book is about: a balanced attack combining an underwritten budget topped by special appeals and other resources.

⹀ 2 ⹀

Budget: A Bad Word
Doing Good Things

Staring at ripening wheat fields in western Oklahoma years ago, I couldn't imagine how that grain was going to be harvested. Those fields stretched to the horizon and beyond. "'Amber waves of grain,'" I said softly. That phrase from Katherine Bates's "America, the Beautiful" described perfectly what I saw. Before writing those words, she must have seen what I was looking at.

How are they going to harvest it all? I wondered. I'd seen only an occasional combine sitting beside the farmers' barns. It didn't seem like nearly enough machinery to harvest those huge fields.

Then, one day on the road I passed a convoy of combines and trucks filled with harvesting crews. Someone explained that these were custom harvesters, mobile crews that start in south Texas as soon as the wheat ripens there. Stripping wheat fields county by county, they work their way northward.

There was my answer. Rather than every farmer having to bankrupt himself by buying expensive equipment that will lie idle most of the year, farmers all over the central U.S. put the same equipment and crews to work. The manpower and machinery of these custom harvest crews do what the individual farmers could not do by themselves.

The reason this system works is that not all the wheat fields in the central U.S. ripen on the same day. Those fields don't even ripen in the same month. In Texas wheat fields begin ripening in the spring. In the Dakotas it's late summer before the wheat is ready to harvest. That's why a small amount of mobile crews and equipment can harvest such huge expanses.

The Bible uses a lot of harvest metaphors. Jesus said: "Open your eyes and look at the fields! They are ripe for harvest" (John 4:35). Another time He told His disciples: "The harvest is plentiful but the workers are few" (Matt. 9:37).

Not surprisingly, it is easy to find parallels in a wheat harvest to Nazarene missionary strategy. One analogy lies in the temporary use of outside workers. In some parts of the world, the gospel message arrives and finds immediate response. The harvest may be ripe, but there are almost no local workers. Elsewhere, the church is quite small. There isn't enough local manpower or other resources to bring in the ready harvest. So we send custom harvesters (missionaries) into those two kinds of fields. These missionaries don't go to homestead a country. Their goal is not to settle down and carve out a permanent place for themselves. There are farmers—the national Christians—who live there, who "own" the land. The missionaries are simply the temporary custom harvesters.

Another wheat harvest analogy is that of right timing. To wheat harvesters, timing is important. Custom harvesters work their way from one field to another, harvesting grain as it ripens. This way, costly equipment and manpower don't lie idle in one area when it is harvesting season in another. The New Testament mentions this right timing for the harvesters (Mark 4:29; Gal. 6:9). As the grain begins to ripen in a particular field, we are called to pour in manpower and other resources to gather that harvest. Or, to continue the harvest metaphor, storms can break over the ripened grain and destroy it in the fields. So, for the sake of those who are responsive and for those who are still unresponsive, we must find ways to give immediate attention to responsive people.

Pooling Resources

Christ has given the Church some awesome commands. "Make disciples of all nations," He told us (Matt. 28:19). We must obey. That we have done so joyfully is typified by Nazarene founder Phineas F. Bresee's statement: "Our church is preeminently a missionary church." It's true. Properly challenged, Nazarenes have never been reluctant at trying to obey the Great Commission. Noted evangelist R. V. DeLong wrote that he was a Nazarene because "the Church of the Nazarene takes the Great Commission seriously."

The Great Commission was given to the Church. Fulfilling it is the responsibility of every local church. How is that possible? Some superchurches might conceivably have the resources to attempt global evangelism by themselves. But, how can your local church do what God has called you to do? How do you dare try to carry out that Great Commission? Simple. By pooling resources with other churches.

Take that word *budget*. The word came from an old French word, *bougette*. To the French it meant pouch or small bag with its contents. That's good symbolism for us. With General Budget we Nazarenes are putting our resources together in one bag. Decades ago missionary pioneer Harmon Schmelzenbach said: "Individually, we accomplish limited returns. Collectively, we move mountains." He was right. Using our budget bag, we run Kingdom activities in more than 95 world areas. Every Nazarene church, no matter how small, has a part in the work of more than 600 missionaries.

During the 1923 General Assembly debate on setting up the General Board and funding it, Rev. L. Milton Williams said: "God and 1 man can chase 1,000 and 2 put 10,000 to flight. What might God and 50,000 Blood-washed, fire-baptized men and women accomplish?"

Once we decide to work cooperatively, we face another question: How to actually raise that money? Suppose we financed day-by-day operations of Nazarene world outreach using individual offerings. We might do that on a country-by-country basis. We could ask every Nazarene church to take an offering for work in Argentina this Sunday, an offering for work in Bolivia the next, and so on. The problem with this is that we work in more countries than there are Sundays in a year. Taking offerings alphabetically by country, we'd never get to Zambia!

Another option would be to take offerings for each area of ministry. We do, of course, promote some special offerings like the Radio Fund and Alabaster for buildings. Suppose that, in addition to these few, we also had to take individual offerings for such things as:

> *Bible Colleges on Six Continents*
> *Church Growth Research*
> *General Assembly Fund*
> *General Superintendents' Global Ministries*
> *Headquarters Support Personnel*
> *Language Study for Missionaries*
> *Missionary Kids' Education*
> *Missionary Salaries and Housing*
> *Missionary Travel*
> *Nazarene Medical Missions*
> *Nurses' Training Schools*
> *Outreach to Unreached Peoples*
> *Passports and Visas for Missionaries*
> *Pastors' and Evangelists' Conferences*
> *Pioneer Districts' Support*
> *Publishing Holiness Literature*
> *Regional Planning Offices*
> *Repairs to Buildings*

Retired Missionaries' Pensions
Support for National Pastors
Thrust to the Cities
Youth Evangelism

In our beginning days, we Nazarenes financed missions with special offerings like that. The first foreign trip by a general superintendent was paid for by a churchwide special offering. In our early years local churches were besieged with requests to take offering after offering for general church ministries. At one early General Assembly, delegates complained that the continual offerings "overdid the matter of solicitation . . . sometimes even cutting pastors' salaries short."

Is there a better way? How can we finance what needs to be done without smothering people with endless offering appeals? Can we assure that the custom harvesters don't run out of gas in the middle of harvesting a field? The 1923 General Assembly delegates felt so. Their answer was to combine all general church ministries into one unified General Board. Rather than every ministry office making its own funding drive, all became part of the new General Board, integrating their offering appeals into one unified General Budget.

Initially, every church was just urged to give liberally to support that General Budget. Then, some districts began setting goals of so much money per member. Finally, in 1949, global evangelism offering goals were linked to local church income. Each local church was asked to aim at giving 10 percent of its income for world evangelism. It would be like a "tithe" given by the churches. When we began this Ten Percent giving emphasis, giving to General Budget and Approved Specials was under 6 percent across the denomination. It has now grown to well over 9 percent. We're closing in on that Ten Percent goal.

Parenthetically, some use the Ten Percent formula to note how incomprehensible it is that less than one-tenth of every dollar given to the local church goes for world missions. They contend that far too much of what they "give to the Lord" winds up being spent on local ministries. Those reaping most of the benefits of "the Lord's money" are actually the givers themselves.

At any rate, to underwrite this budget, a system evolved in which two big offerings, one at Easter and another at Thanksgiving, began raising most of the money. For many churches, Easter and Thanksgiving offerings are highlights of the year. Occasionally I've been in churches that regularly take part of their regular offerings to meet their share of the General Budget. That's a real tithe of the tithe! Others depend less on big offerings at Easter and Thanksgiving, using a year-round giving system called "Faith Promise," where members add something for world missions to their weekly tithe check.

In whatever way it is raised on the local level, General Budget is the key element in putting our custom harvesters in the field. With more than 9,000 churches underwriting this General Budget, we are able to put crews on our harvest combines. Haiti, for instance, is unusually responsive today. We've reaped an incredible harvest in that Caribbean nation, immeasurably aided by our General Budget system of basic funding.

Yet, Haiti's responsiveness does not blind us to other opportunities around the globe. We use our budget-funded system to plan and execute long-term strategies for carrying out the Great Commission. A global strategy funded by General Budget forces us into a balanced view of opportunities and responsibilities around the world. We do not flood one country while ignoring others.

A budget system also offers advantages on the spending end. During periods of retrenchment, a budget system can keep missions going. Working on a budget can nurture a passion for efficiency. That was, in fact, the hope of the General Assembly committee that recommended establishing a General Budget. That committee said one result of a General we've tried coining a new meaning for it. We Nazarenes talk about "paying our budgets." You really cannot do that, however. *World Book* encyclopedia calls budget "a financial plan that helps people make the best possible use of their money." So, a budget is not something you pay.

You can give to the General Budget. You shouldn't say, however, that you've been "assigned a budget." Budgets are not what you're asked to give. Budgets are spending plans. They're not paid or collected. Only the general church can be said to have a "General Budget." That's the plan of how the General Board expects to spend the money it receives in a year.

Your local church has a budget, a local budget. What this spending plan should include are contributions to the General Budget. How much should your church be giving to global ministries? Well, our international operating budget has been divided into more than 9,000 slices. There's one for every Nazarene church around the globe. Some slices are big. Some slices are very small. Each church's financial strength determines the size of that slice. That slice gives your local church a way to fulfill its global responsibilities.

Through the years, we've used all kinds of images to say what we mean by General Budget. Picking up on a lifesaving metaphor, we've called General Budget the "lifeline" for Nazarene missions. Sometimes we've given it human shape, calling it "Mr. General Budget." General Superintendent D. I. Vanderpool talked about meeting this Mr. General Budget in far-flung Nazarene outposts.

Not long ago, I was at the San Antonio District annual NWMS Convention. While there, I joined the District Council members in a skit in which I played Mr. General Budget. That year the district had fallen short of its share of support for the General Budget. As a result, I played a rather sickly Mr. General Budget. Parenthetically, being weak and sickly was good imagery in that situation. General Budget underpayment does reduce our flexibility, forcing us back into a maintenance position. Plans have to be cut back. Strategies for expansion have to be pared down.

Board should be "not a larger, but a more compact organization." Operating on a budget also avoids a stuttering, stop-start cycle of overspending after big offerings and then having to rein in if income drops off.

Some General Budget money has become "seed" money. That is, it helps plant churches that grow from being consumers of the General Budget to being contributors to it. Each new local church started adds to the pool of General Budget givers. Puerto Rico is a good example. Once, it was a mission field. Now, this Caribbean district is a regular one, giving over $25,000 each year to the General Budget.

Budget—Is It the Right Word?

Not all is rosy with General Budget, however. Approach some Nazarenes and strike up a conversation about paying the General Budget. Watch them bristle. They'll likely grouse that their General Budget is too high. Giving that much to global outreach cripples their local church, they say. Why do they feel that way? Well, "budget" sounds ominously like taxes. People fight and howl about taxes. Bad feelings about taxes so distort Nazarenes' view of General Budget that debates about paying the General Budget quickly disintegrate into something more at home in the political arena than in the Kingdom.

The word *budget* sticks in some people's craw not only for its tax overtones. It also may smack of limits. Constant talk of "paying the budgets" even gives some the impression we're preoccupied with money. *Budget* can give the impression that we're more concerned with sustaining an organization than we are with carrying out Kingdom mandates. Just thinking of the word *budget* rather than what it is doing leads to bad decisions when expenses rise above income. When money gets tight in a local church, paying the budgets is often put off. Maintaining the local ministry inevitably takes precedence over an imposed tax being spent on things unrelated to the mission of the local church.

Some of our problems with *budget* may also be becaus

Sometimes we've used military images to promote the General Budget. "General" General Budget is portrayed as leading Nazarene forces invading enemy-held territory. Whatever the imagery, General Budget is these things and more. It's the unifying thread of Nazarene general church structure and global outreach.

To avoid the distressingly negative overtones of the word *budget*, Linda Seaman, missionary to Africa, talks about "Great Commission Investments." A film was even produced using that phrase to explain General Budget. The 1989 General NWMS Convention voted to ask for a name change to "Great Commission Fund." General Assembly delegates did not agree. Still, there are numerous substitutes in use. In central Oklahoma the Cushing Nazarenes use "Eternal Investments." The Joplin District uses "General Investments." In Kentucky it's "Firstfruits." South of Oklahoma City, the Norman Nazarenes call it "Shares for Others."

"Big deal," some of those who think of it as a tax will say. "Whatever you call it, we have to come up with the money. What difference does a name make?"

It makes a difference. People who mistakenly view General Budget as an imposed tax feel powerless and resentful. That's not a good atmosphere in which to raise money for world evangelism. We've got to do a better job of explaining, or else we've got to change our terminology.

Strategic Planning

The General Budget system allows us to follow a strategy in planning the worldwide operation of the church. During World War II, American troops island-hopping across the Pacific often talked of getting a beachhead established on islands held by enemy troops. By this they meant that an invasion force of assault troops would land and throw the enemy off a small section of the beach. Then, they would use that newly conquered small area to bring in troops and supplies for a major effort to wrest that island from the enemy. Having General Budget as the funding core of our cooperative global efforts has enabled Nazarenes to secure beachheads in more than 95 world areas.

Most nations are actually mosaics of peoples. Parts of several of these mosaics are very responsive to the gospel. Some people groups are only moderately responsive. Some are resistant to the gospel. This should not surprise or disturb us. Jesus pointed out that some areas would be more responsive than others.

Over 200 years ago John Wesley studied Britain's social scene. He tried to discern where God's preparatory, prevenient grace was at work. Believing that the Holy Spirit opened certain groups of men and women to God, he chose to proclaim the gospel to those responsive segments of the population. John Wesley was our spiritual ancestor. Like him, we must try to discern where the winds of the Spirit are blowing, then unfurl our sails before them.

Our General Budget system allows us to balance our missions resources between harvesting very responsive fields and the cultivating of unresponsive fields (looking to that day when they will become responsive). Our cooperative General Budget system of raising and disbursing funds avoids unduly favoring those fields generating the best stories or whose missionaries are the best deputation speakers.

Naturally, every area of ministry could use a bigger share of the General Budget than it is receiving. General Budget helps us tailor our response to opportunities so that we meet needs in orderly fashion rather than just jumping in where somebody is yelling the loudest. Dividing up that general ministries fund is not always easy. "By preparing a budget," says the *World Book,* "[we] can make sure that enough money is set aside for items that have the highest priority."

Although we employ a budget system as the financial core of our all-out effort to carry out the Great Commission, it does have certain drawbacks. We have to guard against the insidious tendency to degenerate into institutional survival. Maintenance can replace mission, and we can just fine-tune what we're now doing, improving a bit here and there while ignoring new outreach opportunities. The issue of control also raises its ugly head occasionally. Some of our own recent General Board reorganization sought to steer us away from empire building and turfism.

Cutting Into the Muscle

In the precomputer era, strategic planners used the World Mission office floor. Annual funding requests from all the fields came to Kansas City. These request forms were spread out across the floor of the missions office. The requests included money to maintain current work plus hoped-for expansion. The World Mission staff pored over the cluttered floor, walking around to look, bowing to pray, trying to discern God's will. Dr. George Coulter spoke of the "harrowing experience" of looking at the huge gap between the money missionaries asked for each year and the amounts being given by local churches toward General Budget. Requested amounts were lowered and juggled until the grand total on those request sheets came down to anticipated income. This grand total was the World Mission portion of the General Budget.

Computers now simplify and speed up this process of adjusting and readjusting figures to make authorized expenditures match anticipated income. The process has also been decentralized with details now ironed out at regional centers in cities like Quito, Ecuador; Manila; and Johannesburg, R.S.A. It should be clear how much underpayment of General Budget hurts our global outreach machinery. Any fat that may have been in the original requests from the fields has already been eliminated. General Budget underpayments mean that some muscle has to be cut out.

General Budget is not a tax. It's a way to combine resources to do what would not be possible for any individual church working on its own. Remember Cinderella in the delightful European folktale? Mistreated, abused, and poorly dressed, Cinderella didn't seem to belong in the same family as her lovely sisters. In the end, however, she turned out to be the most beautiful and charming one in her family. I think General Budget may be a Nazarene Cinderella. Disguised by an ambiguous label, General Budget has been reviled, mistreated, and abused. Those of us who know it well, however, see it as something beautiful, helping us fulfill our global mandates.

☰ 3 ☰

We Call It General, but It's Very Specific

I'm trying to become computer literate. At times it's been frustrating. That computer does not always respond as I think it should. Sometimes I suspect my keyboard and monitor take a fiendish delight in defying me.

Stumbling along, I've learned that a good computer will do spectacular things! From the experience I've even picked up a sermon illustration or two. One comes from basic computer technology. You see, without software or programs, a computer is useless. Take away software's complex instructions, and even the most expensive computer is a useless collection of exotic electronic parts.

In some ways Nazarene General Budget resembles a computer's operating system software. General Budget "boots up" or starts our worldwide system and provides an operating environment. It draws together the basic elements of global evangelism and fits them together in an effective manner. Without the structure provided by General Budget, Nazarene world outreach would grind to a halt. To be sure,

General Budget provides only part of Nazarene missionary funding. Offerings like Approved Specials, Work and Witness, Alabaster, Radio, Child Sponsorship, and Hunger and Disaster build on what General Budget is doing. Giving in such special, designated offerings easily arouses more interest and emotion than does paying the General Budget. A whispered temptation comes to let General Budget giving slide while concentrating on some favorite special offering. That would be a mistake. Special offerings, no matter how large or emotionally rewarding, do not pay missionaries' salaries, keep hospital doors open, or carry out strategies on a global scale. Without General Budget we'd revert to spotty, fitful efforts financed on emotional whims.

Where Does It Go?

We say General Budget is for world evangelism. Our colorful posters say: "Missions!" That's why we've urged people to give in Thanksgiving and Easter offerings. Our slogans sometimes lead people to assume that the World Mission Division gets every penny of these big offerings. Forgetting that it is "General" Budget, they express surprise —even dismay—that the World Mission Division does not get every General Budget dollar.

Actually, each General Budget dollar is divided among five ministry areas of the General Board: Church Growth, World Mission, Communications, Sunday School, and Finance. At Nazarene Headquarters, more than 200 people work in these five ministry areas. General Budget pays most of their salaries and funds most of their programs.

The simplest way to explain where General Budget dollars go is with an 80/20 formula. Of each General Budget dollar, about 80 cents goes to missions. The remaining 20 cents is for other general church ministries and overall administration. In stark contrast to what happens in many nonprofit organizations, very little goes to actual fundraising.

Even costs labeled "administration" are sometimes misleading. Take the general superintendents, for example. They are part of the 20 percent administration. Still, Dr. William Greathouse preaching to 3,000 people in Port-au-Prince was probably more "evangelism" than I was on the days I spent double-checking Haitian district statistical reports before mailing them to Kansas City. Yet I was considered "evangelism," and Dr. Greathouse's support was labeled "administration."

A few years ago a general superintendent was in Haiti, holding district assemblies. He heard about a young pastor's wife who was seriously ill. Three hundred dollars of medical bills had far outstripped that struggling family's resources. Unless past due bills were paid, she would get no more medical help. When that general superintendent departed Haiti, he left behind $300 to wipe out those bills. The fund he used that day was a part of the General Budget labeled "general administration." So even some of those expenses labeled "general administration" could well be called "world evangelism."

Not everyone is happy with the 80/20 disbursement plan. Some complain that too much money goes overseas. There is so much yet to be done at home, they argue. We're top-heavy in foreign missions spending, they say. Others see immense numbers of unsaved in the far corners of our world. They lament that we can't do more in evangelizing unreached peoples.

Another problem with a simplistic 80/20 explanation is that internationalization has blurred the lines between "us" and "them," between home and foreign. It isn't "us" here and "them" over there anymore. It's not just one or two countries giving the money, sending all the missionaries, making all the decisions. We're now all in it together. The only "them" are peoples outside the gospel message, in whatever country they may be. Because of that, the five divisions of our Headquarters are moving to try to serve all areas of the church on six continents.

This is reflected in the way funds go to world mission-administered districts. Take publications, for instance. In earlier years, literature funds went through World Mission office. Now Publications International works directly with national leaders around the world.

The Specifics of General Budget

While "budget" may be somewhat misleading, its adjective "general" may also be inaccurate. We use general to mean inclusive, but it also can mean broad or nonspecific. Actually, General Budget works in very specific ways. Here are some explicit things General Budget does:

■ MISSIONARIES. The food for more than 600 active Nazarene missionaries, the rent for their homes, and the gasoline to run their vehicles comes from General Budget. We call it *General* Budget. It seemed pretty specific when we used it to do things like sending our children, Matthew and Rachel, to school in Italy and then Haiti.

The late General Superintendent J. B. Chapman dreamed of having 1,000 Nazarene missionaries on foreign mission fields in time to celebrate our church's golden anniversary. That anniversary celebration was in 1958. We haven't yet reached Dr. Chapman's visionary goal. Still, through 80 plus years, more than 1,800 people supported by Nazarene missionary giving have served as Nazarene missionaries. They've heralded the Good News in places like Pretoria, Paris, and Pago Pago. Amazingly, one-third of those missionaries are still active. In our short history 33 missionaries have each given more than 40 years of service.

Some missionaries evangelize and plant churches. Some missionaries train national pastors and evangelists in Bible schools and extension programs. Then, we've also always carried a concern for the whole person. That's part of our heritage as a Wesleyan movement. So General Budget also supports some medical missionaries. They oversee Nazarene medical ministries that treat more than 300,000 patients a year. You'll also find an agricultural missionary or two as well as some construction experts. You'll find missionaries involved with primary and secondary schools run by the Church of the Nazarene. Some run vocational schools.

With Christ's second coming on our minds, we hurry to complete the task. With some urgency, we work as though He is coming back tomorrow. Yet we also have a long view, knowing that we may not view time and history with God's eyes. So while we search for ways to get as many missionaries on the field as possible, we also look ahead for the missionary. When missionaries do retire, we intend to care for them. So there's a missionary retirement plan funded by General Budget. There's also a General Budget-supported missionary retirement complex in Temple City, Calif., where retired Nazarene missionaries live.

Our way of supporting missionaries with pooled resources beats any other I've seen in action. Missionaries in some groups raise their own support. That is, they get people or churches to pledge so much per month for them individually. That money goes through their home office, where a percentage of donations will be taken out for administrative and publicity costs.

In the fall of 1974 we arrived in Italy as rookie missionaries. We got acquainted with another newly arrived American family. As missionaries with an independent board, they raised their own support. During their year of language school, a couple of their supporting churches changed pastors. The new pastors wanted to help different missionaries. Funds that had gone to our friends were redirected to other missionaries. As a result, when language school ended, our friends returned to the United States to spend several months raising more support.

Ten years later in Haiti, we got acquainted with another independent missionary couple. They spent nearly two weeks of every month producing a monthly newsletter and writing personal letters home. The reason? To raise enough funds to be able to minister the last two weeks of the month. They liked to boast that every dollar given to their work got to the field. It did. Yet, they spent half their time raising the next month's support. In all honesty, their fund-raising expenses should have been calculated at 50 percent of their income.

General Budget eliminates those problems for Nazarenes. Nazarene churches do not send a few dollars each month to specific missionaries. Rather, donors give to General Budget. That fund supports all 600 Nazarene missionaries. As a result, while our missionary friends in Italy left for home after language school to raise more support, we moved into our place of ministry. While our friends in Haiti were forced to spend half their time raising money, we were full-time missionaries.

Every army has supply or support troops that back up the frontline soldier. The Nazarene army is no different. General Budget puts support or supply troops behind Nazarene missionaries. Their work frees the missionaries to do what they went overseas to do. That is, in fact, the principle laid down in Acts 6:2-4. Faced with overwhelming work loads, the Early Church leaders wisely set up a support team. Thus, the apostles were freed from time-consuming ministries only marginally related to their specific calling. Aided by these support troops, they gave themselves wholly to their original ministry.

Our support troops include people in the Nazarene World Mission Society office who produce mission education materials, coordinate prayer support, and facilitate fund-raising. Through mission education programs they encourage children and young people to consider the missionary call.

The support troops also include a World Mission Division deputation secretary who makes up speaking schedules for furloughing missionaries. Setting up a year's worth of deputation services can be complicated. A furloughed missionary doing deputation will speak in 150 to 200 services during the year. A deputation secretary saves the missionary endless hours of letter writing, high overseas telephone bills, and poring over calendars. A secretary's work frees the Nazarene missionary to spend his time in cross-cultural ministry.

Another support person provided by General Budget is the World Mission Division finance manager. He gets finances to the field. He makes certain that full accounting is given for every dollar. One of his assistants helps missionaries prepare their income tax returns. Others process visa applications and ship equipment and supplies. These people all help make the missionary on the field as productive as possible. We might call support people our "Acts 6 missionaries."

■ RADIO, TELEVISION. General Budget helps to fund Nazarene radio broadcasts around the world. We now produce regular programming in 40 languages and dialects. Fifteen hundred stations carry these programs to listeners in almost 100 countries, some of them closed to missionaries. Some of the needed funds come from the annual NWMS Radio Offering. That annual August offering now brings in nearly $750,000. While that's a substantial sum, it's not enough. So General Budget adds additional funds.

Radio is only part of what we're doing in electronic communications media, however. General Budget enables us to produce outreach, training, and publicity materials in media formats ranging from audiocassettes to video productions.

As missionary in residence at Southern Nazarene University, I use such Nazarene-produced films as *They Cry in the Night, The Calling, An Alabaster Heart,* and *The Master's Sheep* to motivate and instruct future missionaries. Each month videotapes go from Headquarters to missionaries on the field carrying information, greetings, and highlights of general church gatherings. General Budget provides all this.

■ LITERATURE. The Church of the Nazarene works in more than 50 languages. Nazarenes speaking each of these languages need good holiness literature. We publish books, Sunday School literature, tracts, and magazines in languages whose names I can't even pronounce. In some languages we don't yet have a lot of churches and members. Therefore, sales are limited. To keep prices affordable, literature production must be subsidized. General Budget picks up that subsidy tab.

■ **NATIONAL LEADERSHIP.** I often get asked: "What did you do as a missionary? Did you pastor a church?"

Few Nazarene missionaries pastor churches. We couldn't possibly send out enough missionaries to pastor every Nazarene church around the world. In Haiti, for instance, we have 300 churches. To put missionary pastors in all those churches, we'd have to transfer our *entire* Nazarene missionary force into Haiti (and that still wouldn't be enough pastors).

Missionaries have unique roles to play, but there aren't enough of them to complete the task of world evangelization. They only start the job. Finishing the Great Commission task will be gifted leaders from every tribe and people group. That's why General Budget develops and supports national leadership. These are not paid lackeys. We are helping gifted, Spirit-filled men and women make their dreams for their countries come true.

Barbara and I served in Italy for about 10 years. Today, competent Italian Nazarenes lead the Church of the Nazarene on that European peninsula. Because the district is small, General Budget helps support the district superintendent. In the Caribbean, few of Haiti's 300 Nazarene churches get outside support for their pastors. District superintendents' salaries in Haiti are, however, subsidized by General Budget. Such strong Nazarene leadership is emerging around the globe. With General Budget support, people of many tribes and tongues are leading Nazarene world outreach.

■ **LEADERSHIP TRAINING.** Your General Budget giving prepares pastors, evangelists, and leaders for holiness ministries around the world. Through Nazarene schools General Budget helps prepare leaders who will keep us true to our heritage as part of the Wesleyan holiness movement. General Budget monies support about 40 Bible colleges. We are working to set up a university in Africa. Five thousand students study at these schools in both resident and extension programs.

General Budget's help in developing strong national leadership includes even the United States and Canada. There, General Budget has subsidized PALCON conferences for pastors and WILCON conferences for women in leadership.

General Budget help reaches to include Nazarene Bible College in Colorado Springs as well as its 16 extension centers across the United States. General Budget helps support two graduate seminaries. One of these is in Manila, training leaders for Asia. The other one is in Kansas City.

You may protest, of course, that U.S. and Canadian churches take special offerings each year for Nazarene Bible College and for Nazarene Theological Seminary. These offerings build buildings and care for other capital improvements. They don't, however, pay salaries or the light bill or buy books for the library. Some of these items are paid for from tuition; General Budget also picks up a hefty share of the costs.

■ THRUST TO THE CITIES. Fourteen cities in our world each have 10 million or more people in them. Forty-six others each have more than 4 million. Such megacities are special mission fields all by themselves. Our major missions thrusts in the 21st century will be in the battle for the souls of these cities.

We've planted a lot of churches in small towns and villages around the world. Still, working in the large cities is not new to Nazarenes. A burden for the cities took root in the organizational meeting of that first Church of the Nazarene in Los Angeles. The minutes of that October 30, 1895, meeting include the statement: "The field of labor to which we feel called is the neglected quarters of the cities."

Our campaign to evangelize the cities centers on our Thrust to the Cities program. Each year, one or more world-class cities is highlighted. Basic funds for these thrusts—be they in Berlin, Paris, São Paulo, Toronto, or Chicago—come from General Budget.

■ GENERAL SUPERINTENDENTS. Support of our six general superintendents, who are important elements in Nazarene world outreach, comes from the General Budget. Back in the 1920s Nazarene leaders decided that a general superintendent would preside over all Nazarene district assemblies everywhere. This put all districts worldwide on equal footing. It was a major step whose effects would finally burst upon us in the 1970s with internationalization.

The president of the Italian Evangelical Association told me that our general superintendents amazed him. Elio Milazzo said that within a few hours of stepping off a plane in Rome, they seemed to have a handle on difficult problems. He said he had not seen other Americans grapple as effectively with local problems as do Nazarene general superintendents.

The general superintendents' concern for adequate resources to accomplish our God-given vision is typified by the late J. G. Morrison. As this general superintendent talked to Nazarenes about giving to the General Budget, he was well-known for his plea: "Can't you do just a little bit more?"

Decision-makers. Preachers. Even fund-raisers. That's what general superintendents are. They're much more, however. As they give direction and inspiration to our denomination, the general superintendents create the networks that hold us together. They're counselors for missionaries, district superintendents, college presidents, and pastors. More than once I've cried on their shoulders.

Our balanced fund-raising attack funds a balanced leadership team. Adding to the effectiveness of our general church are other leaders like the general secretary, general treasurer, and education commissioner. They, too, form a ministerial support team like the one in Acts 6.

■ YOUTH MINISTRIES. Each summer nearly 300 Nazarene young people are involved around the globe in Youth in Mission. In 1987 a gathering of 4,000 Nazarene young people in Washington, D.C., included our son, Matthew. While the young people themselves raise a good deal of money for these events, they are also aided by General Budget support. From this pool of young people will come lay leaders, pastors, evangelists, and missionaries.

I think back to the 1962 International Institute in Colorado. I was one of that crowd of Nazarene teenagers. Paul Orjala, pioneer missionary to Haiti, was one of the speakers. His messages and presentations helped solidify my sense of call. General Budget subsidy for that event may have been called an *expense*. It was actually an *investment* in future world evangelism.

Our General Budget investment in youth pays early dividends. Through the years Nazarene youth have gotten involved in special missions offerings. Nazarene beginnings in Alaska, Australia, and Germany were all funded with special Nazarene youth offerings. Youth groups often go on mission trips, raising all the needed money.

At the 1989 General NYI Convention, it struck me that within 10 years those young people could be major contributors to the world evangelism effort. As they move into their careers, they will be deciding how to get involved, if at all. How would we reach them? Later that summer we were at Nazarene Day at King's Island near Columbus, Ohio. I saw Nazarene young people proudly wearing their "Dare to Run," "Radically Saved," and "Share His Spirit" T-shirts. I wondered: As they move to adulthood, will they adopt a radical Christian life-style? Will they make significant resources available for world evangelism? Or will they be seduced by satanic materialism? The General Budget investment we're making in Nazarene youth can help push them toward a radical Christian life-style.

■ HELPING LOCAL CHURCHES. Headquarters ministries like the Sunday School Ministries Division and the Church Growth Division help local churches expand and improve their ministries. Workshops. Conventions. Seminars. Materials. All are helpful to local churches. They all, however, cost money. These are often subsidized by the General Budget. In a recent year, for example, Evangelism Ministries held 29 schools of evangelism. Each month, Nazarene leaders receive *Insight,* a newssheet spotlighting church growth trends.

During our 10 years in Europe, we always made time to go to Germany for the annual European Nazarene Servicemembers Retreat. Each year, American servicemembers and their families—about 200 in all—gather in the Bavarian Alps for that week-long retreat. I remember altar services where service personnel who had grown up in Nazarene churches got back to the Lord. I remember testimonies of sanctification. Part of the funding for this retreat and one in Asia comes from General Budget.

■ GENERAL ASSEMBLIES. The Church of the Nazarene is a big family. Our quadrennial General Assemblies make that clear. We love getting together. Still, General Assemblies cost money. It costs money to rent convention centers and stadiums, to print ballots, and to pay secretarial help.

The 1989 General Assembly heard reports from commissions studying the call of a pastor, Nazarene higher education, and the God-called evangelist. It takes money for these commissions to meet, research, and write recommendations for the assembly. It takes money to get Headquarters staff to the General Assembly. General Budget money picks up those bills.

"We can't afford not to"

One Wednesday night recently I spoke at Wichita, Kans., First Church. It was the opening of their annual Faith Promise Convention. Wichita First is a church that often gives more than 20 percent of its income to missions. At the close of that service Pastor Gene Williams stepped forward to explain their yearly goal. He explained where monies would go. He told how it would be going toward the General Budget, to two planned Work and Witness projects, and to several Approved Specials. As Rev. Williams came back to the total goal, he hesitated. Then he said: "Folks, we can't afford not to reach this goal."

He reminded them of the church's earlier financial troubles. Those had been severe. The problems had, however, evaporated when members radically increased their giving to General Budget and to special missionary projects. God blesses obedient churches just as He does obedient people, Rev. Williams said.

Occasionally I hear someone moan and groan because a church has been asked to make larger budget contributions (based on its increases). Not long ago I was in Loveland, Colo. In one service of that missions weekend Rev. Gary Abke was praising the Lord. He had just calculated Loveland's General Budget assessment for the next year. It was going to be higher. He didn't moan and groan over the increase. Rather, he was brimming with excitement about the larger share expected of them for world evangelism. As he talked, someone down on the third row said, "Praise the Lord!" The congregation had caught his enthusiasm.

At a Gallup, N.Mex., Faith Promise Convention banquet, Pastor Tom Crider said: "I've got good news and bad news. Here's the bad news: The General Board is recommending lowering General Budget assessments. That means they'll be asking less of us for world evangelism." He paused.

"That's bad!" Rev. Crider continued. "Now here's the good news: we'll be able to overpay our General Budget by larger amounts than we have in the past!" I like Tom's spirit!

God's call to take the Kingdom message into all the world is clear. Each local church must obey on its own, or churches can band together, pooling their resources with other local churches. We Nazarenes have chosen to do it together. We call our primary financing method "General Budget." It's been nearly 70 years since its launching. It took a while for the idea to catch on. But it did. Then, along the way we discovered that we didn't like our bread plain. We wanted something on it. So we began to add some specific offerings to our General Budget giving. That is, however, the subject for another chapter.

≡ 4 ≡

Peanut Butter and Jelly

One evening I was bumping down a dirt road hugging Haiti's south coast. Destination? Damassins, a small village where we had a new church. Few villages in rural Haiti have electric power. All I saw dispelling darkness along the road was an occasional oil lamp or flickering candle. When I reached the edge of Damassins, I saw a bright light ahead. That puzzled me. I didn't think there was electricity in that village.

Someone must have a small generator, I thought. Then, as I got closer, I saw that the light was coming from our church. Shining so brightly that dark, moonless night was not an electric light bulb. It was a Coleman lantern hanging from the rafters of the brush arbor. As I walked into that brush arbor, I remembered that Approved Special money had helped Damassins buy a Coleman lantern. Our global outreach underwritten by General Budget had helped plant that church. Approved Specials had provided something extra.

Coleman lanterns work by burning pressurized kerosene on a carbonized cotton mantle. I don't know why that produces such a bright light, but it does. One Coleman lantern gives off as much light as *two* 100-watt light bulbs.

Sure, Haiti's churches could survive without Coleman lanterns. Many Haitian congregations use only smoky little oil lamps. While dispelling a little darkness, those oil lamps are only slightly better than a candle. Even with one of them beside me on a pulpit I've struggled in vain to read my Scripture text. A Coleman lantern changes all that, giving a new atmosphere to night services.

Through the years we've helped lots of Haitian churches by subsidizing their purchase of a Coleman lantern. General Budget would have never stretched far enough to include those lanterns. Fortunately, we run a balanced fund-raising attack. With General Budget underwriting the core of our global strategy, we've moved creatively to find more resources.

The 1920s' switch from using specific emotional appeals for everything to a comprehensive budget financing most areas of general church ministry almost killed Nazarene missionary outreach. Nazarene giving to missions plummeted overnight. A sinking treasury caused all kinds of curtailments. At the end of General Budget's first year, the General Board heard some dismal reports. Then-treasurer J. G. Morrison said it had been "the saddest year that the foreign missionary cause of the Church of the Nazarene has known." Eventually, however, Nazarenes rallied to the idea of giving to a budget system. Now, many churches actually overpay their assigned share of the General Budget.

Still, having General Budget as the only way to give to missions wasn't satisfactory. Not long ago I saw a bumper sticker that said: "Man doesn't live by bread alone; he needs peanut butter and jelly as well." The bread for Nazarene world outreach is General Budget. But we've discovered we don't like it plain. So, through the years, ways to add emotional appeal offerings to General Budget giving have emerged. We've put peanut butter and jelly on our basic bread.

Among the potent extras we've added are Approved Specials. Often raised by NWMS, these special offerings provide tools for missionaries and leaders in their evangelistic efforts. District teen and children's NWMS groups are always raising money for an Approved Special. Approved Specials come from Sunday School classes or children's church groups. Through the years, NWMS has been very creative in raising money for Approved Special extras. I've often thought that a colorful addition to Nazarene Archives would be a collection of posters, banners, and other props that have been used to raise Approved Special money for our missions outreach.

Why the "approved" label? Every year, mission fields send proposed specials lists to the World Mission Division office for approval. These lists look like Christmas wish lists. On those lists will be vehicles, medical equipment, construction tools, literature, and scholarships. On those specials so approved by the Ten Percent Commitee, churches can receive credit toward Ten Percent giving.

I saw Approved Specials help Nazarene outreach in Italy and Haiti. Today, thanks to Approved Special giving, Italian Nazarenes have their own hymnal. Equipment used to publish Italian literature came from Approved Special giving. Approved Special funds provided a tent for evangelism in Italy. Folding chairs used in the tent and in Sunday Schools across Italy came from Approved Specials. Rural pastors in Haiti ride Approved Special horses and mules up to mountain villages where the gospel has never been preached.

How do people find out about these specials? One way is through *World Mission* magazine. Almost every issue highlights a few Approved Specials. However, *World Mission* can only devote so much space to such special needs. Even if the editor made room, you wouldn't wade through several pages of those requests every month. A recent issue had a list of

11 items from countries in our Asia-Pacific Region. That was about 1 item from each country's list. So while most requests sent in by districts and Mission Councils get on the "approved" list, few of them get published in our monthly magazine.

Even though the full lists never get published, they're available for the asking. At your request, World Mission office will sift through them to find exactly what interests you. Or you can ask about a specific country, and they'll send you its entire specials list. You also can mention the total dollar amount you have in mind, and someone from the World Mission office will make up a list for you with several items in that price range. You may also contact your district NWMS president for special projects.

Ten Percent Giving

Ten Percent credit is given not just on General Budget and on Approved Special requests from the field, but on several other items as well. The Ten Percent Committee of the general church preapproves each item. On that pre-approved list are North American multicultural ministry projects. It includes giving to Nazarene student ministry centers and some North American church planting projects. It includes giving to Nazarene military coordinators in World Mission areas as well as support funds given to college students in the Youth in Mission programs.

Ten Percent credit is also given for:

■ Alabaster offerings
■ Missionary deputation offerings
■ Nazarene Compassionate Ministries
■ World Mission Radio offerings
■ Authorized Work and Witness projects
■ Medical Plan
■ LINKS
■ Missionary Christmas Fund
■ VBS Offering

Bequests

Another peanut butter and jelly item we put on our General Budget bread is that of deferred giving, or bequests left by people who have gone to be with the Lord. We've received such help in our own missionary ministry. For years, Edith Lantz worked in youth publications at Nazarene Headquarters. She edited Sunday School lessons for junior high pupils and spoke in Sunday School conventions across the United States. She was also a driving force behind Nazarene youth programming prior to and following World War II.

Edith Lantz was my wife's aunt. Toward the end of her life she asked that the money from the sale of her house and car would go into improving Christian education. We've used those funds in our work with Christian education as missionaries. Edith Lantz has been gone 20 years. When she was alive, she never visited a mission field. Today, however, her influence continues in Christian education endeavors on mission fields. Through finances her estate is providing, her giving goes on.

She's not alone. Many people want their ministry to continue even after they die. When they make out their wills, they leave part of their estate for world evangelism. These amounts—many of them somewhat modest—allow General Budget dollars to stretch farther than seems possible. Altogether, annual bequests to various Nazarene ministries now top $20 million. About one-fourth of that, or $5 million each year, goes to missionary projects.

Interested in leaving a legacy like this? Making out a will is not very complicated. The Nazarene Planned Giving office at Headquarters has field personnel in most areas of the U.S. and Canada. They stand ready to help you at *no cost or obligation.* If you use their services, you will not be pressured to leave something to the church. It can be, however, for you a final act of stewardship that helps fulfill the Great Commission.

Occasionally, people make the World Mission Division the beneficiary of a life insurance policy. This happens most often when someone discovers an old forgotten paid-up policy. Since they were not depending on it, they change the beneficiary to the World Mission Division.

Sometimes families set up memorial funds, asking that friends give to a specific project on a mission field instead of sending flowers. As an example, the family of E. G. Benson, longtime Sunday School promoter, set up a memorial fund to train rural pastors in Haiti. What a special way for Christians to add to our balanced attack.

Deputation Finances

Normally, Nazarene missionaries spend four years on the field and then one year back in their home country. During this year of furlough they speak in what we call deputation services. That word *deputation* symbolizes our General Budget approach to world evangelism. It refers to the office of deputy or delegate, to someone acting on someone else's behalf. Using this word is significant because Nazarene missionaries on furlough are not raising their own individual support. While we report on our own work, we also represent the whole Nazarene missionary force. We are, in a sense, raising support for more than 600 missionaries. Hence, the word *deputation.*

Our main aim is reporting on behalf of the missionary force, to boost interest in the whole missionary program. Still, as we travel from church to church, congregations will take special offerings for us.

Like Approved Specials, these offerings count toward Ten Percent giving. Every dollar given goes to that particular missionary's ministry. The only fund-raising costs are the missionary's travel expenses to get to the particular service. Everything above those expenses helps that missionary buy equipment or pay certain living expenses.

Money from deputation offerings provided Barbara and me with vehicles and tools, typewriters and washing machines, automotive repairs and tires, projection equipment and sound systems, and ham radio equipment for communication.

There were never any "administrative costs" taken out. General Budget picks up those administrative costs. That's another reason it makes sense to channel all your missions giving through the Church of the Nazarene. When you give to other groups, you'll usually wind up paying administrative costs again.

Medical Plan

We missionaries have no divine guarantee of a healthy life. Early Protestant missionaries to tropical Africa rarely lived long enough to learn the local language, let alone return for a second term. A coffin was an essential part of their equipment. That's no longer true. Still, over the past decade health risks have increased for missionaries. New problems include virulent and resistant forms of malaria and hepatitis.

The quality of medical care has, of course, risen. So have costs. Charges for emergency and routine medical care for missionaries have, in fact, skyrocketed so much that medical bills, plus the missionary retirement plan, now consume *10 percent* of each year's annual World Mission Budget. Even before General Budget came along, a Medical Plan fund was set up to help care for these costs. That particular offering was not absorbed into General Budget (although since 1983 increasing amounts of General Budget money have had to be used to supplement that medical fund). With General Budget help and receipts from Memorial Roll and Distinguished Service Awards, the Medical Plan offering helps missionary families cover the costs of:

- diagnosis of little-known tropical diseases
- dental, eye, and ear health care
- evacuation by air ambulance from remote areas
- physical exams at furlough times

- childhood illnesses and broken bones in missionary kids
- health insurance for MKs in college.

That medical fund cared for me when I got hepatitis in Haiti. It cared for me on furlough when I injured my leg with a chain saw. It cared for my wife, Barbara, when she had nerve damage repaired in her hand. It cared for our children, Matthew and Rachel, when they got malaria in Haiti.

Prayer and Fasting

Two years after General Budget started, the Prayer and Fasting League was begun. The idea was simple: Fast a meal. Spend the time in prayer. Give the price of the meal as an offering. Way back then, some churches used that money to pay church debts. A few raised building funds using the Prayer and Fasting idea. Some went so far as to pay pastors' salaries from it. Still others gave it to missions. Within a short time, however, the General Board voted to unify the Prayer and Fasting League behind a single purpose: pray, fast, and give for foreign missions. For some local churches today, Prayer and Fasting giving plays a key role in their General Budget giving.

Special Occasion NWMS Offerings

Every so often the NWMS will sponsor a churchwide special offering. Our work in both New Guinea and Venezuela got under way with just such offerings. The NWMS silver anniversary project was an offering for Bible schools. Such special, onetime offerings have included hospital construction. The latest of these offerings was the 75th anniversary special for Hong Kong and China.

Each year there's also an offering to give each missionary a cash gift at Christmas. The annual Radio Offering boosts our use of electronic media in evangelism and church planting.

Our Artillery Salvos

Some time ago I sat talking about mission finances with Doug Tatton. A Canadian, Doug served in Haiti with another denomination. For a while he was their field director. While in Creole language school together in Port-au-Prince, Doug and I became close friends. As we talked that particular day about organizational structure and denominational missionary strategy, I explained how our General Budget giving is amplified by Approved Specials, Alabaster, deputation, and other similar offerings. His church lacked that double-barreled system. He had to try to squeeze everything out of one unified budget similar to our General Budget. They had to plan for everything far in advance. Ours, on the other hand, is a system of basic budget plus extras as the Lord provides. Our balanced attack encourages a certain amount of spontaneity and direct emotional involvement. It gives people the chance to respond directly to certain needs. It does provide that feeling of knowing exactly where your money is going. It also avoids some of the problems of putting everything into a unified or General Budget. It is a good system. It helps protect our commitment to outreach, encouraging us not to allow institutional demands to subvert our mission to unreached areas.

We often joke about all the offerings Nazarenes take. I don't apologize for those offerings. Nazarenes enjoy giving. I like the balanced way we do it.

≡ 5 ≡

The Nazarene Construction Company

I sometimes wish all churches didn't have to pour precious resources into bricks and mortar. Unfortunately, congregations don't usually stay small enough to meet in living rooms (or else people don't build big enough living rooms!). Though they may start in homes, they soon need larger spaces for worship, ministry, and evangelism.

In affluent countries, providing buildings isn't an insurmountable problem. When churches in the United States and Canada want to build, they usually visit a local bank. There, they get a loan with a 15- or 20-year payback period. Though it may take 20 years to pay off the loan, the church goes ahead and builds the building and gets to use it.

In most other countries of the world, however, churches cannot get such loans. Construction often must be done with hard cash. Before it can be used, the building must be paid for. That's a problem. Building on a strictly pay-as-you-go basis is difficult in the U.S. and Canada. In countries where the average annual income runs under $1,000, having to pay cash for building projects can be an insurmountable hurdle for a local church. Unfortunately, with our growth around the world, General Budget doesn't have enough in it to provide buildings. What to do?

Alabaster

Remember those Alabaster march offerings every February and September? When I was a kid, we'd put a cardboard box shaped like a church on the altar. Singing a song, we'd all march down front. We'd break the paper seal on our Alabaster boxes and empty them into that cardboard church. At box-opening time others would add checks or cash.

That began several years ago when the Lord inspired Elizabeth Vennum with an idea built on the biblical story of the Alabaster container of perfume poured over Jesus' feet. The missions offering that Elizabeth envisioned was to come from discretionary money, from what we could decide to spend on perfume, not from what we would be spending on food. Perfume is put on for our own pleasure. With no sacrifice we could live without some of it. Mrs. Vennum's idea for Alabaster was to challenge Nazarenes to do without a *want* to satisfy a *need*. Alabaster offerings were to come from money we had originally planned to pour out on ourselves, but then we chose instead, like Mary, to pour it out on Jesus. When a person wanted something extra, he would give it up and put that money in a little cardboard "Alabaster" box. That money would be for buildings on mission fields. Many churches still have march offerings in which they empty the little boxes into the big Alabaster church.

In giving Alabaster offerings, occasionally churches do some creative things. Recently, for instance, in Shreveport, La., First Church the people were raising 62,000 pennies for their Alabaster offering. They had a five-gallon glass jar they were filling with those pennies.

Alabaster goes 100 percent for buildings and property. One could make a case for using a little bit of each Alabaster dollar for administrative costs. But not one penny is used that way. General Budget absorbs those costs. Every bit of Alabaster money goes to missions. Eighty percent goes to world mission and 20 percent to multicultural ministries in the U.S. and Canada.

Since 1949 we've raised $38 million in Alabaster. With that we've built more than 3,000 churches, parsonages, clinics, missionary homes, educational buildings, and camp meeting centers. The $2 million now coming in each year from Alabaster is a significant addition to our balanced attack.

In Haiti, Work and Witness meets most construction needs. Still, Alabaster money buys property in Haiti, including most recently an entire church and parsonage!

Here's what happened: For years we had helped the congregation in Limbé to rent property. For one reason or another, the landlord was always on the verge of evicting the congregation. A couple of times he even boarded up the building, forcing the district superintendent to make emergency trips to negotiate a solution. We were also having to rent a parsonage there. The Nazarene elementary school was trying to hold classes in the sanctuary. Students had only the pews to sit and write on.

The church began looking for land on which to build. What they found was too expensive and poorly located. They looked for buildings that could be renovated into church buildings. Nothing excited our imagination.

Then, an independent pastor in Limbé decided to close his church and leave the ministry. He personally owned both the church and parsonage. While that may sound a bit strange, he was like some American televangelists whose ministry is theirs personally. Because he was moving to nearby Cap-Haïtien, he put his church building and parsonage up for sale. The price was something we could manage with Alabaster funds, so we helped the church buy it. Today, because many Nazarenes sacrificed wants to meet needs through Alabaster, the Limbé Church of the Nazarene has a fine building on the main north-south road in Haiti.

Work and Witness

Where have Work and Witness teams been? The list would read like a list of the airline hubs of the world: Manila, Nairobi, Mexico City . . .

Sending work teams has become a major missions thrust for districts and many local churches. These people give up vacation time to work. They buy their own airline tickets. They even dig into their pockets to buy cement, paint, nails, and boards. In recent years, they've put up hundreds of buildings all over the world. A grass roots program, Work and Witness moved into high gear with the election of Paul Gamertsfelder to the General NWMS Council. Now, over 300 teams go out each year.

Louie Bustle is now regional director in South America. Originally the pioneer leader in the Dominican Republic, he has credited Work and Witness with being a key element in explosive church growth there. Work and Witness money and the donated labor are key elements in helping General Budget reap a great harvest in responsive areas around the globe. In many fields Alabaster funds buy land, and Work and Witness teams put up the buildings.

Sometimes a team's construction materials money is raised through special offerings. Occasionally money comes from friends outside the church. They hear about special projects and want to get involved. Sometimes, churches use Faith Promise giving above General Budget commitments to help fund Work and Witness projects.

One "Acts 6" missionary support team member in the World Mission office is the Work and Witness coordinator. Some years ago, David Hayse moved from overseeing construction in Mexico to become the first full-time Headquarters coordinator for Work and Witness. His notebook bulges with a backlog of pleas from mission fields asking for construction teams.

Rev. Hayse helps sort out priorities, matching teams with projects. He helps schedule teams for the field. He double-checks important details such as accident insurance. David Hayse doesn't live on a mission field. Yet, he is making a difference in Nazarene building projects around the globe. His being on the job is due to General Budget.

People often ask me: "Wouldn't it be better if we just sent the money? With local labor couldn't you get the building up for less cost? Isn't buying airline tickets and paying for food and lodging for Americans a waste of missions money?"

No! A thousand times no. First, without a team involved we know we wouldn't get much of either the travel money or the materials funds. It's easy to motivate people to give when they are personally involved. Because they themselves are going to work on that project, they give generously to buy the materials, something they would not otherwise be nearly as excited about doing. Buildings go up that would not be financed on appeals for money alone. Second, as for the airline ticket money, that is usually vacation money. People are going to spend that on themselves. Then, third—and possibly most important—is the fact that these trips transform the feelings of team members about missions. Inevitably, they become lifelong missions supporters.

Besides groups there are also one-member teams who pay their way to a mission field to give specialized expertise for short periods. David Hayse keeps a computerized "skills bank" listing of people who are willing to give their time and skills where needed.

Memorial Chapels

Some people dream that a rich relative will die someday and leave them lots of money. They dream about all the things they would do with that money. Such dreams rarely come true. When they do, however, some Nazarenes choose to do something significant on a mission field rather than spending all the money on themselves.

One Nazarene family in the northwest U.S. has received inheritances from both sides of the family. Both times they used the money to build churches on a mission field. One of those is in Ounaminthe, Haiti. That church and parsonage stand as a testimony to two lives given over to Jesus. While the Haitians benefiting from the memorial gift do not know the family who helped them, the buildings they use testify daily not only to the work of Christ in the life of the person who has passed on but also to the deep commitment of the one who, upon receiving the inheritance, gave it to the Lord.

These memorial gifts increase the effectiveness of General Budget dollars. Sometimes they are the key to finishing construction projects where a Work and Witness team could not raise all the funds to buy needed construction materials.

General Budget. Approved Specials. Alabaster. Bequests and Memorials. Radio. Work and Witness. What an impressive array of channels God uses to get Nazarene resources to the battlefront. And that's not all. There's even more.

≡ 6 ≡

I Was Hungry and You Gave Me Something

One afternoon I was huffing and puffing my way up a mountain trail in southern Haiti. That Saturday, District Superintendent Evens Grammont had me in tow. The trail led toward two new churches we planned to visit Saturday night and Sunday morning.

Occasionally, the trail widened into a primitive road. Noticing that, I asked Rev. Grammont about it. He explained that the two churches we were going to visit had organized volunteer road-building gangs. One morning a week, villagers along that trail turned out to hack a road into that mountainside. About all they had, he said, were machetes. Could we help them buy a few shovels and maybe even a wheelbarrow? Fortunately, I could say yes.

Even when they've finished, those villagers won't have much of a road. It'll just be a dirt trail chopped into a mountainside. Still, four-wheel-drive vehicles can soon get to those villages. A road will make it possible for those rural Haitians to get farm products to market and sick people to hospitals. They'll be able to get building materials back to their village. An access road also increases the chance that the government will help with education and health needs.

I've never said much about buying those shovels and that wheelbarrow. That's unfortunate. I'm convinced that the more Nazarenes know what their missions dollars are doing, the better off we'll be. Unfortunately, our publicity machine often putts along in low gear.

Occasionally I meet Nazarenes who are having second thoughts about having sent money to some relief organization about which they knew very little. Slick advertising caught their attention. Wanting to help, they dug deep into their pocketbooks. Later, they wondered if they'd been wise in their giving.

Pictures of starving children can tug at your heartstrings. Living conditions in third world countries can be wretched. Every three days hunger kills as many people as would a small nuclear bomb. Maybe you've sent money somewhere because such a need touched you. Even while mailing your check, however, you wished that your church was doing something to meet that need.

What services should Nazarene Compassionate Ministries be providing? Feeding programs? Public health? Sanitation? Potable water supplies? Economic development? Road building? Agriculture? Good news. We're doing all that.

In more than 95 world areas, evangelism is our primary thrust. As we herald the Good News, we find ourselves compelled by Christ's love to reach out to people with physical needs. That's part of our Wesleyan heritage. As a result, we're probably involved in almost anything you want to give to. Nazarene Compassionate Ministries money has even gone into places like Ethiopia, Poland, and Soviet Armenia, where we do not yet have any churches.

Many groups begging for your relief dollars have high fund-raising costs. Those have to come out of your gift. These costs, plus their administrative expenses, reduce the amount of your gift actually going to the need. The Church of the Nazarene is different. Some of our special offerings go

100 percent to the need. These include Alabaster, Radio, Work and Witness, Medical Plan, Missionary Christmas Fund, and Approved Specials items. All fund-raising costs and administrative expenses for these come from General Budget.

Our Compassionate Ministries funds are handled a little differently. Some administrative costs are taken out of these offerings. Even then, our fund-raising costs are minimal. For one thing, most fund-raising is done by volunteers from local NWMS groups. More than that, General Budget pays many of the administrative expenses of running Nazarene programs. Missionary salaries are just one example of this. Why pay those costs again? Funnel your giving through the Church of the Nazarene. Don't pay administrative costs twice!

Hunger and Disaster Fund

One of the newest elements of our balanced attack is the Nazarene Hunger and Disaster Fund. Money raised for it lessens immediate suffering from disasters such as earthquakes and hurricanes. Hours after such tragedies strike, Nazarene Hunger and Disaster funds can be there.

Yet, natural disasters aren't the only things causing human misery. There are also places in this world where people cling to the very margin of existence. Hurricanes or earthquakes aren't their main problems. Victims of a distorted global economy, they're stranded in the backwaters of a world rolling toward the 21st century. Just day-to-day living is for them one continuous disaster. By helping eliminate chronic malnutrition and pervasive poverty, the Hunger and Disaster Fund aims to make a significant, permanent difference in those people's lives.

Haiti is a good example. It is probably the poorest country in the western hemisphere. While Hunger and Disaster money has intervened at famine times, it also finances hog-raising projects. We've started vocational schools in India. These hog-raising projects and vocational schools seek to wipe out chronic poverty and hunger by tearing at their roots. In a recent year Hunger and Disaster money provided help in 300 relief and development efforts.

Where does this money come from? Individuals sometimes make onetime gifts to the Hunger and Disaster Fund. Some churches give offerings to the Hunger and Disaster Fund. Hunger and Disaster money extends and amplifies the evangelism and compassionate ministries funded by General Budget.

Child Sponsorship

In its first four years, Nazarene child sponsorship plans attracted 6,000 sponsors. Several child sponsorship plans form a family of programs under the Compassionate Ministries umbrella. They are helping Nazarene children in 34 different world areas. Benefiting are war orphans in Guatemala, malnourished children in Haiti, Native American children, and pastors' children around the world. The children are Nazarene children. The programs are run by Nazarene missionaries and national workers.

Child sponsorship or other compassionate ministries offerings should never, of course, replace General Budget support. They are, however, another source of funds for our balanced attack.

═ 7 ═

Giving More with Less Pain

Our third furlough began in late summer of 1988. We arrived in Bethany, Okla., in time for the Northwest Oklahoma District Assembly. Following an evening service, Judy Duey came hurrying across the sanctuary of Bethany First Church to greet me.

"Do you remember that Faith Promise Convention you held in Mountain Grove?" she asked.

I did. It had been 10 years earlier, during our first furlough from Italy. I had known Carl and Judy Duey in college. So I stayed with them that weekend. They were starting their family. They were also building a house in that small southern Missouri community.

Giving to missions in a regular, systematic way through Faith Promise was new to Mountain Grove Nazarenes. It was new to Carl and Judy. The idea is to use a monthly or weekly approach to giving funds to carry out Christ's Great Commission.

Carl and Judy hesitated to commit themselves to such regular missions giving. They had young children and a house under construction. They felt financially strapped. The tithe was the most they felt they could spare.

I only spent a weekend in Mountain Grove. Monday, I left that little town, not knowing what Carl and Judy had decided about a Faith Promise commitment. It sounded like they had decided to forgo giving until a more rosy future arrived and they could make the kind of financial commitment they'd like to missions. I hoped that, as a result of our conversations, they would at least make a token commitment. My deep prayer, of course, was that they would reorder their financial priorities to make what would be for them a substantial Faith Promise. Ten years went by. Here, standing in front of me, was Judy Duey.

Did I remember that weekend in Mountain Grove? "Of course," I told her.

"Well," she said, "that first year, the Lord got our money. Then, the second year, He got our lives."

Carl and Judy spent two years in Swaziland working at the hospital there. Then they spent two years in Malawi starting a vocational school. The Faith Promise approach to missions giving had literally revolutionized their lives.

How Faith Promise Works

Most Spirit-filled believers would like to give more to missions. Tragically, for many Christians, missions offerings are relegated to bothersome intrusions. At the mention of a special missions offering, they scramble to see how much can be spared from their checking account. Sadly, it's often less than they would like.

One solution has been Faith Promise, a system of weekly or monthly giving. In Faith Promise, missions giving—like the tithe—comes off the top of one's income rather than having to be salvaged from leftover money at the end of the month. People often find they give more to missions when they do it on a weekly or monthly basis than they do when they give only a few major offerings during the year.

Churches using Faith Promise plan a special Sunday or even weekend each year. In a special service, people commit in writing what they feel God wants them to give to world evangelism during the coming year. Faith Promise commitments are usually given on a weekly or monthly basis, depending on when the person gets paid. People are urged to step out on faith, to go beyond what might seem possible, to make a *faith* promise. Often the total of these promises is announced in that commitment service as part of a victory celebration.

The primary goal of Faith Promise commitments is, of course, to help the local church meet its share of the General Budget. Many churches who use Faith Promise have discovered that they've been able to do more than just meet their share of the General Budget. To their joy and amazement churches sometimes discover they can give to missions more than twice the amount of their General Budget share.

Life-style or Interruption?

One advantage of the Faith Promise system is that people's involvement in missions will become an integral part of their life-style, as it did with Carl and Judy Duey. Not everybody will wind up on the mission field as the Dueys did. Still, I pray that supporting global evangelism will be for you more than a bothersome intrusion that comes along occasionally and sends you scrambling to see what your checkbook balance is.

If you are on Faith Promise, one way of making missions more than an intrusion is to use your check-writing time to pray for world evangelization. As you make out that check each week or month, pray that God will use those resources in extraordinary ways to reach the unreached. Prayer, after all, is the primary thing we need. Money given without prayer commitment means that giving will eventually dry up. If, on the other hand, the prayer support is there, the financial support will also be there.

Faith Promise can help you rearrange your priorities in financial matters. Do you want Jesus in first place? Then your life—finances included—should reflect His priorities. Rearranging your financial affairs to free up more financial resources for the Kingdom makes a strong statement to your family, to others, and to God.

Rev. Marvin McDaniel, pastor of Greenville, Tex., Peniel Church, says he finds that Faith Promise helps people become tithers. New people get excited about giving to missions through Faith Promise. They see how God blesses faithful stewardship. By the second year they've begun tithing as well.

Conscious Decisions

For some families, Faith Promise has meant putting off major purchases for themselves. Not long ago I was with an Indianapolis family who had planned to buy new drapes for their home. Those new drapes were to have cost about $1,500. Then that family got so excited about missions giving that they delayed buying draperies for a year. Five years later the old drapes still hung in that home. That family had fulfilled Elizabeth Vennum's dream for missions giving. They had given up a *want* to meet a *need*.

Far too many Christians live as though the Kingdom has signed a peace treaty with satanic forces. We lavish on ourselves everything that God puts into our hands. As a result, we've missed what He's trying to do through us. Christians need to adopt a warfare life-style. That means living modestly and simply, in keeping with the demands of soldiers actively engaged in spiritual warfare.

Some time ago someone sent me a newspaper clipping about a Baptist family who had sold their luxury house. They moved into a mobile home where their monthly payments for housing would be considerably less. The reason? To have more money to give for Kingdom purposes. North Americans are usually trying to buy the biggest house and most expensive car they can afford. They get tied in knots by mortgage payments, car payments, and every other kind of payment. As a result, they don't have much uncommitted income to channel into missions. To move to giving significant amounts to the Kingdom, they must slash their monthly payments in some drastic way as that Baptist family did.

Through Faith Promise some people wind up giving more than what they had originally promised. During our first furlough, I was with a pastor in Iowa. The year before, he had made an unusual Faith Promise. He had promised the Lord that extra money of any kind that came his way during the year would go into Faith Promise. It was a rather open-ended commitment that included windfalls of any kind. Among these extras would be the honoraria that people sometimes give pastors for weddings. Incredibly, in that one year, the Lord put $7,000 extra in his pocket. True to his pledge, he put it all into Faith Promise.

Giving More with Less Pain

I'd encourage you to set a goal of the percentage of your income you will give to Kingdom purposes. This would include your tithe, building fund pledge, missions, and revival meeting offerings. Let's say you'd like to be giving one-fourth of your income. Maybe as you look over your checkbook register for the past year, you see that you're now giving 12 percent. It might take some draconian measures to jump in one year to that 25 percent level. Instead, why not try moving up in graduated increases? Begin by adding 3 percent to your annual giving to Kingdom purposes. Do this each year until you reach your goal. In this way, incremental adjustments can be made smoothly in your family's living standards. Another way to move up to a higher percentage of giving is to let salary increases help you. When you get a raise, continue to live on what you've been getting all along. Put the extra into Faith Promise.

I often meet people who earlier in life felt a call to full-time Christian service. For one reason or another they did not go overseas. They feel guilty about settling for what they believe is God's "second best." Yet, I often discover they aren't giving much above their tithe to the Kingdom. What a shame. Money represents our time. So just by raising the amount of their financial giving, these people could be giving significant amounts of their time to missions. They really did miss the Lord's will! Not only years ago but also today.

Sense of Sacrifice

Faith Promise does help most people give more money to missions. But being able to give with less pain—even if it's more—also has its drawbacks. Rev. Michael Hancock pointed that out during a Faith Promise Convention at Tulsa, Okla., Regency Park. He commented on how much his family now gave through Faith Promise. Then somewhat wistfully he said he missed that sense of sacrifice he remembered as a youngster.

Back then, his family gave a week's salary in the Thanksgiving offering and again at Easter. He talked of how they cleaned out the refrigerator around those special offering times. They couldn't buy any groceries that week because they'd put all their weekly income into the missions offering. Some meals were mighty lean, but there was a deep sense of satisfaction at having given in the spirit of Christ. We need some creative thinking to find ways to keep that sense of sacrifice in our missions giving.

Lack of Education

In addition to a loss of a sense of sacrifice, Faith Promise can eliminate some mission education opportunities in a local church. "Faith Promise makes us careless in educating people," said Carla Hurt at a recent Michigan District NWMS Convention. Each of the special offerings of our balanced attack offers an opportunity to teach about Nazarene world outreach. Such education must continue even when regular Faith Promise giving provides the funding.

When they enter a Faith Promise program, some churches completely dispense with special missions offerings. That's a bad idea. First, when pledges fall short of a goal, it's often because only a small percentage of the potential givers have participated. The members of that church have accepted Christ. Many haven't yet accepted His Great Commission. If no special missions offerings are ever taken, these people who haven't made Faith Promises will coast through the year without ever being challenged again to give to missions.

Then, we must also be sure that we're allowing the Holy Spirit enough opportunities to speak to us about giving our financial resources to fulfilling the Great Commission. When Barbara Stroud was NWMS president on the North Arkansas District, she reminded churches using Faith Promise not to drop special offerings during the year. She said: "People still need opportunity to be led by the Spirit in inspirational giving." Even Faith Promise needs that balanced approach of an underwritten budget and inspirational giving.

Rev. Dale Coble leads the Larned, Kans., Nazarenes in Faith Promise giving. They still, however, take all the individual offerings through the year. He continues with special missions emphases and offerings at Thanksgiving and Easter, when a furloughed missionary comes to visit, as well as offerings like Alabaster, Radio, and Medical Plan. Promoting each of those offerings keeps missions awareness high in the congregation.

Still another problem with Faith Promise is that churches using it rarely *overpay* their General Budget commitments. In the past, overpayments by some churches with large Easter or Thanksgiving offerings made up for those churches that fell short.

Recently, I was with a pastor friend whose church had suffered some financial setbacks. A sagging economy had caused a population exodus. Fortunately, their aggressive outreach program had kept attendance from dropping. Still, these newcomers to the church had not yet reached the same level of sacrificial giving as had the departed old-timers. For the first time in his 20 years of pastoral ministry, my friend was going to district assembly with an unpaid General Budget commitment. He was carrying a heavy load of guilt over that lack.

I tried to console him by reminding him that other Nazarene churches would be overpaying their share of the General Budget. Thus, where he had fallen short would be covered by someone else. Unfortunately, with large numbers of churches on Faith Promise, fewer General Budget over-payments are being made today than in previous years. Churches are raising more money; they're just channeling it into areas like Approved Specials and Work and Witness.

Faith Promise is one method some churches are using to be a part of every area of our balanced fund-raising attack. Properly used, Faith Promise could add real punch to the contribution your local congregation is making to fulfilling the Great Commission. My hope is that it will enable increasing numbers of churches to overpay their share of the General Budget while also giving generously to other areas of our balanced attack.

≡ 8 ≡

Doubling and Tripling Our Investments

How much are you now giving to missions? Would you like to give two or three times that much? Good news. It's already happening! How? Well, every dollar you give to General Budget is being multiplied. Let me give you an example. Some time ago, I sat in Port-au-Prince, Haiti, reading the weekly mail. I opened an envelope from Bible Literature International. Out fluttered an $8,000 check. Stunned, I grabbed the letter and began to read. The check was for us to buy 10,000 New Testaments.

Sometime earlier I had run across Bible Literature International's name and address. As mission director, I wrote to ask for help with Scripture portions to use in evangelism.

BLI president Jim Falkenberg wrote back. They had a backlog of pending requests, he said. However, he did ask me to send a proposal describing what we could use, and our plan of distribution. When I got his letter, I thought: Why not ask big?

So I wrote him a proposal for distributing 10,000 Creole New Testaments. We could buy those New Testaments in a paperback edition for 80 cents each from World Home Bible

League. Amazingly, that cost even included shipping into Haiti. I asked Bible Literature International for $8,000 to purchase those 10,000 New Testaments.

Months passed. I heard nothing. I decided our request had been for naught. Then, here came Jim Falkenberg's letter: "Enclosed is a check for you to purchase 10,000 New Testaments."

Holding that check, I sat dumbfounded. How could these people trust us? They didn't even know us! Or so I thought. Later, I discovered they worked with Nazarene missionaries in several other parts of the world. Not only that, but several employees in their Ohio head office were Nazarenes. They did know us. They knew we could be trusted.

General Budget put us on the field. This group then channeled the distribution of 10,000 New Testaments through us. Furthermore, a year and a half later they came back and gave us the funds to purchase 15,000 more! General Budget money didn't buy those New Testaments. This wasn't even Nazarene money. Yet, it was multiplying the effects of Nazarene General Budget money.

Hot Lunches Multiplied

Missionary Bill Dawson is in charge of our Compassionate Ministries in Haiti. Every year, in the late spring, he used to sweat a bit. You see, that's when TEAR Fund let him know if they would be helping our Haiti hot lunch program for the following year. TEAR Fund, based in Great Britain, is the relief arm of the European Evangelical Alliance. Its name comes from the first letters of the words "The Evangelical Alliance Relief." For several years they poured nearly $100,000 annually into feeding Nazarene schoolchildren in Haiti. Suppose they decided at the last minute not to continue helping us. Where would we find the money to feed those children? You can understand why Bill worried.

They did eventually phase out that aid. But for years, they came through. TEAR Fund people trusted us. The relationship was perfect for both groups. They wanted to help children. Nazarene schools in Haiti have lots of children: 25,000 of them. The TEAR Fund didn't have to spend its money putting staff people in Haiti to oversee and direct a feeding program. General Budget pays many of the administrative costs such as maintaining missionaries on the field. By picking up some of those costs, we got an additional $100,000 annually. General Budget funds were being multiplied.

Compassion International, a large Christian child sponsorship organization, pours in even more money to Nazarene schools in Haiti. They spend close to $300,000 annually helping with Nazarene schools, multiplying what General Budget money is doing. They are helping in similar ways in India and other countries.

When people give to Christian organizations, one of their concerns is how much of the money winds up at the need. Nazarenes need not worry about that. For us, it's not a question of how much will get there. Rather, it's a question of how much multiplication will occur along the way!

Free Buildings

In the fall of 1987 we spent an evening with an independent missionary family working in Haiti. During the meal, missionary Art Clauson dropped by. As we talked, he asked if we had any use for a Butler metal building.

Art, who serves with the Church of God, told us that a company in Canada had ordered four large prefabricated buildings from Butler, Inc. These were buildings using large steel arches covered on the roof and walls by painted sheet metal. Butler built the buildings as ordered. Then, before the ordering company took delivery, it went into bankruptcy. Butler found itself with four custom-made buildings and no customer.

Someone within the Butler organization convinced the company to donate these buildings to a nonprofit, charitable organization. Those buildings went to the Christian

Reformed church, which then began looking to give them to someone working in Haiti.

Just prior to that, we missionaries in Haiti had been tossing around some ideas on expanding our clinic/dispensary building. Only a year earlier we had doubled the floor space of that clinic. Now, with greatly increased numbers of patients, we needed even more space. We also needed classroom space for our new village health worker program, plus more office space. Unfortunately, we hadn't come up with a satisfactory expansion plan. Nor did we know how we would raise the funds for construction once we figured out what we wanted to build.

Then, out of the blue came this offer of a building. We began sketching ideas to use it for solving our space problems. It quickly became clear that this $30,000 Butler building would give us more floor space than we had dared dream about.

General Budget put us in Haiti. We were running a medical project and carrying out other programs. Thus, we had a valid need for this building. The new building, which surprisingly was a two-story structure, also had room for a large X-ray machine that a Nazarene layman in California purchased in a bankruptcy sale. Not only did we get the building, but we were able to supply it with some new equipment. God is multiplying Nazarene resources in unbelievable ways. He's on a "matching" basis with us!

Free Literature

The year 1988 was very special for Nazarenes in Haiti. A 12-month evangelism and expansion push in Haiti launched a Caribbean Region island-by-island focus. The major goal was to reach 95,000 full members in the Caribbean by 1995. Haiti's special year of emphasis was 1988. District superintendents and missionaries in Haiti set all kinds of goals under an umbrella theme of "Haiti '88." These goals included opening work in 88 new villages, running eight citywide crusades across Haiti, organizing two new districts, and ordaining 28 new elders.

As we began gearing up for Haiti '88, I knew we could use large quantities of literature in those special outreach efforts. I remembered a group called Scripture Gift Mission. While in Italy, we had excellent relations with their British office. They had supplied us with hundreds of tracts and Scripture portions in Italian.

So, I wrote their Canadian branch to see if they could help us in Haiti. They responded that 1988 was their centennial year. In 1988 they were going to celebrate 100 years of existence. So, they were looking for some special project to celebrate those 100 years of ministry.

Ultimately, we agreed on several programs to distribute 100,000 Scripture portions. That meant 1,000 portions of Scripture for every year of their existence. They trusted us. Scripture Gift Mission has worked with Nazarenes in several different countries for many years. They knew we would use the literature exactly as agreed.

General Budget funds made possible the big Haiti '88 push. With funding assured for the basic program, we were able to attract lots of other resources, including those 100,000 Scripture portions from Scripture Gift Mission.

Non-Nazarene Work and Witness

Work and Witness has been a tremendous part of our balanced attack. Hundreds of Nazarenes have experienced the Lord at work on a mission field.

To Nazarenes on some mission fields, Work and Witness means more than just Nazarene groups. Other groups believe in what we're doing. So they send teams to help on Nazarene projects. A couple of years ago a Reformed church group spent a week in Haiti, building benches and pulpits for several Nazarene churches. Youth for Christ has been especially helpful to us in Haiti. A dormitory on the campus of Haiti Nazarene Bible College stands as an example of their contributions there.

General Budget giving put a full-time Work and Witness missionary in Haiti. Thus, we can respond when other groups offer their help. Scott Hannay, our Work and Witness missionary in Haiti, recently talked with LeTourneau University in Longview, Tex., about their bringing a group to that country.

Most of these examples come from Haiti. I've lived and ministered there. I know the details of Nazarene work there. Look elsewhere around the world where we're at work. There, too, you'll quickly discover many ways God is multiplying the Nazarene missionary dollar. Because you give, other groups and organizations are willing to invest in Nazarene missions.

In the early 1980s two missionaries in Haiti, Steve Weber and John Burge, made some proposals to the Alberta provincial government. As a result, we got a grant of $75,000 for medical, nutrition, and well-drilling projects. Earlier development projects headed by Walter Crow and the late Charles Morrow helped channel thousands of non-Nazarene dollars into Nazarene efforts.

In one recent year Compassion International sent $1.3 million worth of medical supplies through Nazarene medical work in Haiti. Those supplies were shared with a dozen other organizations who have medical work. We, of course, had first pick for our health center and rural dispensaries. These supplies helped stretch General Budget dollars earmarked for medical work.

So don't hold back. It's not just the $1.00 you're giving. In the end, that $1.00 may wind up being $2.00 or $3.00. Some marvelous multiplication is going on. It's all part of our balanced attack.

☰ 9 ☰

Cleaning Out Garages
and Attics

My toolbox contains a very special screwdriver and pair of pliers. Work and Witness team members from Northeast Oklahoma gave them to me while we were working together on the Moncalieri church in northern Italy. I treasure those tools. They served me well in Europe and in the Caribbean. Every time I see them, I remember Richard and June McGuire from Tulsa, Okla.

When we moved to Haiti, I soon discovered that what the McGuires did was not particularly unique. Work and Witness teams headed to a mission field often put tools and equipment in their suitcases. They'll use them on that job, then leave them for use on future construction projects.

These tools are emblematic of an important aspect of Nazarenes' balanced support of world evangelism. This one involves giving too. This time, it's not the giving of dollars or time. It's the giving of belongings.

Ransacking Other People's Attics

Years ago members of the Nazarene World Mission Society began tearing cotton bedsheets into strips and rolling them into bandages. Nazarene medical facilities around the world still need these cotton bandages that NWMS members make from old sheets.

This giving of textile materials to world evangelism has mushroomed into shipments weighing in the thousands of pounds. In one recent year 12 oceangoing containers, each carrying 4 to 6 tons of used clothing, were shipped to Nazarene mission fields. These containers went to Mozambique, Malawi, Nicaragua, Costa Rica, and Honduras.

On a smaller scale, Work and Witness teams that go to countries often empty their suitcases as they leave. When they go home, they take only the clothes they're wearing. What they leave behind goes to pastors and to needy families in the country where they've worked. United States churches getting new choir robes sometimes send their old ones for use by Nazarene choirs in other countries.

In Haiti, this giving of material goods means empty pill bottles. We get lots of them (and use lots of them). Giving material goods means people collecting sample medicines from doctors and sending them to us (making certain they're not past expiration dates!). Medical supply companies wanting to do a good deed (while also getting a tax write-off!) willingly donate supplies and equipment. Alert Nazarenes have snatched up those supplies and equipment for Nazarene mission fields.

I Love a Parade!

For Haiti and other countries this giving of material goods has meant musical instruments. My involvement with these began during our 1983-84 furlough. In California Rev. Charles Brightup asked if we could use an accordion to take to Haiti. I never turn down anything. So we took that accordion to Haiti. There I discovered that the accordion is the Haitian churches' primary musical instrument. So I gave Rev. Brightup's accordion to a church needing one. Then I began writing everyone we knew or could think of to ask for used accordions. That letter-writing campaign netted us more than 50 used accordions. Those accordions would have had a retail value in excess of $10,000. What a tremendous addition to our balanced attack!

A lady in Oklahoma bought an accordion 25 years before, hoping to learn to play. She never got around to it. When she recounted this story to me, I told her that 25 years earlier she just thought she was buying that accordion for herself. The Lord already had His eye on it for Haiti!

Haitian churches also use other instruments. Some have bands that play not only in church services but also in frequent parades. Prof. Harlow Hopkins at Olivet Nazarene University heard of Haiti's need for musical instruments. Going through ONU's band storage room, he found several unused but good band instruments that he shipped to Haiti.

As I've spoken to Nazarenes about Haiti's need for musical instruments, people have given me not only accordions but also:

Trumpets	Flutes
Trombones	Banjos
Baritones	Guitars
Clarinets	Drums
Saxophones	even a Tambourine

My mother has been my volunteer "instrument packer." In a recent two-year period she prepared more than 250 parcels of musical instruments for shipment to Florida. From there, Missionary Flights International took them to Port-au-Prince on one of their weekly flights. The retail value of all those donated instruments? Over $25,000.

At Enid, Okla., First Church, Rev. Jim Cooper rejoiced with his people at the end of their 1988 Faith Promise Convention. They had pledged nearly $30,000. That weekend they had also given an accordion, two trumpets, and a guitar. In the evening service the Faith Promise thermometer on the platform had those musical instruments grouped around it.

The Miracle Jeep

In 1982 Larry and Martha Wilson went to Haiti as Specialized Assignment personnel. One of their prayers as they held some deputation services before leaving was for money to purchase a four-wheel-drive vehicle in Haiti. As they came down to their last service, their hopes for a jeep began to fade. They hadn't raised nearly enough money. Without a miracle in that last service they were going to fall far short. Undaunted, Larry and Martha committed to the Lord what seemed an insurmountable hurdle.

After that last service in New England a couple approached them. They asked if the Wilsons needed a jeep. This couple had a nearly new one. During the service they had felt impressed to offer it to Larry and Martha as a gift. Praising the Lord, Larry and Martha took the keys and drove the jeep to Florida for shipment to Haiti.

Through the years, other cars have been given to the World Mission Division as part of estate settlements. Even real estate has been given for world evangelism. Naturally, these kinds of gifts may eventually be sold to get money to plow into evangelism. They originally came as possessions, however, and not as cash. What a help they have been in carrying on Kingdom work of helping the blind to see, cleansing the lepers, and preaching the gospel to the poor.

Warranty Service on an Old Copier

Returning to Italy after our first furlough, we took with us a used photocopier. Colorado Springs Trinity Church had given it to us. During our second term of service that SCM copier made copies for the Italy District, for the Italian literature ministry, and for the Florence local church. We didn't have the money to buy one. Through the generosity of a local church, the Lord gave us that one.

That copier was like most machines. It would occasionally break down. Parts for it were not available in Italy. What we needed then was not cash, but parts. Stepping in to find and send us those parts free of charge was a Nazarene family in Salem, Oreg. In one sense, therefore, our copier had come with a warranty covering parts—although we didn't know it at the time. The work of the Kingdom in Italy continued to advance because of the multichanneled giving of Nazarenes in North America.

Wedding Bells

Not long ago Caribbean Regional Director James Hudson led a drive to get wedding dresses for Haiti. People from all across the United States emptied cedar chests. The reason?

Well, when people get converted in Haiti, one of the things they do in straightening up their lives is to get legally married. Churches often plan mass wedding ceremonies on the same day as a baptismal service. In Dr. Hudson's special drive, more than 100 used wedding dresses went to Haiti for new converts' weddings. Many of these are now hanging in closets at district offices across Haiti. They'll be loaned out again and again to local churches. During our last furlough, I got several more wedding dresses given to me by people who had heard of Haiti's need for them. We didn't keep good calculations, but I'm sure the value of the wedding dresses sent to Haiti would be in the thousands of dollars. They've been a significant addition to our balanced attack.

LINKS

Five years after the Texas merger that formed the Church of the Nazarene, the Southern California District began a box work program. The idea was to ship boxes of personal supplies to missionary families. Headed by Mrs. Paul Bresee, this idea was officially sanctioned on a denominational level by the 1921 NWMS Council meeting.

About 15 years ago, to better personalize our missions program, box work was expanded into LINKS. Those letters stand for "Loving, Interested Nazarenes, Knowing and Sharing." For two years at a time the general NWMS office assigns missionaries to a district. For many churches, LINKS has meant a chance to lovingly pick out a few things at the store and send them overseas to a missionary family. Some of our children's biggest thrills come in opening parcels sent by people we had never personally met. Through LINKS we've made a lot of friends we've not yet seen.

Check Before You Ship

All these kinds of gifts—which are tax-deductible as charitable giving in the United States—increase the effectiveness of General Budget dollars. Before packing up and shipping anything, however, you should write or talk to the general NWMS office or to the missionaries on the field. Customs regulations in some countries make it impossible for people there to receive parcels. In other countries, high fees make it impractical. You don't want to cost the missionary more trouble and expense than the item is worth. So check first.

Our balanced attack includes more than money. Each year it also gets thousands of dollars of supplies and equipment shipped to mission fields.

Conclusion

I've always loved Nazarene General Assemblies. The first one I remember attending was in 1960. I was 13 years old. I sat there in Kansas City's Municipal Auditorium, enthralled. I recall looking down on the delegates with dismay as they agreed to raise the church voting age from 12 to 15. That day, they took my voting rights away. Still, I loved it all. One of my favorite areas was the exhibit hall. There were displays from countries around the world. In 1903 Dr. Phineas F. Bresee wrote: "The impulse of the sanctified heart ... is to preach the gospel to every creature." That seemed very evident as I wandered through that display area.

Four years later my teenage faith swelled again. I went to Portland, Oreg. There I marveled at the huge numbers of Nazarenes at another General Assembly. Very few organizations in the world have business meetings where 800 delegates go, accompanied by 50,000 spectators. That happens at our General Assemblies. It's obvious we're a family. I liked being part of something big, where so many people join hands to carry out the Great Commission.

God has used the Church of the Nazarene in marvelous ways around the world. Thousands have come to know Christ and the power of the Holy Spirit through our movement. The holy life-style of the people called Nazarenes has influenced the lives of countless thousands. Part of the driving force behind our tremendous outreach and accomplishment has been an aggressive evangelistic spirit. A good deal of the credit goes to our two-track missions giving system.

General Budget has been the lifeblood. General Budget

has sent missionaries to the field. It has opened Bible schools. It has put up clinics and dispensaries. It has put together a support team at Headquarters. Nazarenes worldwide give to General Budget to support our common missionary task. That's not all. General Budget has been balanced with Approved Specials, Alabaster, Radio, Work and Witness, Deferred Giving, and other extras.

Through the years, we've done some experimenting to elicit the resources to fulfill the Great Commission. Naturally, we still have weaknesses we're looking to shore up. On the whole, however, our balanced fund-raising has some awesome strengths. We've tried to keep our attack balanced. We've worked hard at increasing our attacks on satanic strongholds.

When we went to Italy in 1974, one of the things I had to give up was football. Italian schools do not play football. Back then, there was never a football game on Italian television. I could not interest anyone in the neighborhood in a touch football game in the park. Soccer, maybe. But not football. While I was sad to leave football behind, I did discover an even better balanced attack, that of Nazarene fundraising for missions.

If in the future we are to fulfill our part of the Great Commission, we must see an even greater commitment of funds than we have ever seen. We must do it. I believe we can. Elizabeth Vennum has been instrumental in NWMS fund-raising through the years. Recently, she wrote we could respond in three different ways to a God-given challenge:

1. Do less than you can.

2. Do what you can *without* God's help. He will *let* you do it.

3. Under His direction, in faith, attempt more than you can do alone. Then He will help you do it.

This third option is the story of Nazarene giving for global evangelism. It's not been a few wealthy givers who have made that difference. Rather, those motley collections of day laborers, short-order cooks, and widows called Nazarenes have given sacrificially to "pay" their General Budget and provide all those other extras. It's often been a widow's cruse of oil approach. Trusting the Lord, Nazarenes have poured out to Him what He has given them. It has been a balanced attack, and it has worked.

Board should be "not a larger, but a more compact organization." Operating on a budget also avoids a stuttering, stop-start cycle of overspending after big offerings and then having to rein in if income drops off.

Some General Budget money has become "seed" money. That is, it helps plant churches that grow from being consumers of the General Budget to being contributors to it. Each new local church started adds to the pool of General Budget givers. Puerto Rico is a good example. Once, it was a mission field. Now, this Caribbean district is a regular one, giving over $25,000 each year to the General Budget.

Budget—Is It the Right Word?

Not all is rosy with General Budget, however. Approach some Nazarenes and strike up a conversation about paying the General Budget. Watch them bristle. They'll likely grouse that their General Budget is too high. Giving that much to global outreach cripples their local church, they say. Why do they feel that way? Well, "budget" sounds ominously like taxes. People fight and howl about taxes. Bad feelings about taxes so distort Nazarenes' view of General Budget that debates about paying the General Budget quickly disintegrate into something more at home in the political arena than in the Kingdom.

The word *budget* sticks in some people's craw not only for its tax overtones. It also may smack of limits. Constant talk of "paying the budgets" even gives some the impression we're preoccupied with money. *Budget* can give the impression that we're more concerned with sustaining an organization than we are with carrying out Kingdom mandates. Just thinking of the word *budget* rather than what it is doing leads to bad decisions when expenses rise above income. When money gets tight in a local church, paying the budgets is often put off. Maintaining the local ministry inevitably takes precedence over an imposed tax being spent on things unrelated to the mission of the local church.

Some of our problems with *budget* may also be because

we've tried coining a new meaning for it. We Nazarenes talk about "paying our budgets." You really cannot do that, however. *World Book* encyclopedia calls budget "a financial plan that helps people make the best possible use of their money." So, a budget is not something you pay.

You can give to the General Budget. You shouldn't say, however, that you've been "assigned a budget." Budgets are not what you're asked to give. Budgets are spending plans. They're not paid or collected. Only the general church can be said to have a "General Budget." That's the plan of how the General Board expects to spend the money it receives in a year.

Your local church has a budget, a local budget. What this spending plan should include are contributions to the General Budget. How much should your church be giving to global ministries? Well, our international operating budget has been divided into more than 9,000 slices. There's one for every Nazarene church around the globe. Some slices are big. Some slices are very small. Each church's financial strength determines the size of that slice. That slice gives your local church a way to fulfill its global responsibilities.

Through the years, we've used all kinds of images to say what we mean by General Budget. Picking up on a life-saving metaphor, we've called General Budget the "lifeline" for Nazarene missions. Sometimes we've given it human shape, calling it "Mr. General Budget." General Superintendent D. I. Vanderpool talked about meeting this Mr. General Budget in far-flung Nazarene outposts.

Not long ago, I was at the San Antonio District annual NWMS Convention. While there, I joined the District Council members in a skit in which I played Mr. General Budget. That year the district had fallen short of its share of support for the General Budget. As a result, I played a rather sickly Mr. General Budget. Parenthetically, being weak and sickly was good imagery in that situation. General Budget underpayment does reduce our flexibility, forcing us back into a maintenance position. Plans have to be cut back. Strategies for expansion have to be pared down.